Beading

(TRAVEL EDITION)

PROCESS Journal™

Seed Bead Graph Paper

LOOM/SQUARE STITCH

with **ROUND** beads

Created and Designed by

Cheri Taliaferro Jewelry

Burly Books Publications
SALIDA, CO

Published by Burly Books Publications 2020
First edition; First printing.

Layout design, graphics and writing
© 2020 Cheri Taliaferro

BurlyBooks.com
BurlyBooksPublications.com

Cover image from Shutterstock: Epitavi

ISBN 978-1-951560-05-8

Hi there, Beader!!

We are so happy for you to have gotten your hands on one of these Beading `PROCESS` Journals! Now you can keep all of your creative bursts in one place, and you no longer have to hunt around the web for "free" downloadable beading paper.

This particular travel-size journal accommodates designs for **loom/square stitch with round beads** all in one place! We have also inserted discreet lines for easy counting. This journal has 62 design pages with a blank page on back for drawing or sketching. (We also love the fact that if you choose to color in your patterns with marker or dark pencils, it won't bleed through to the other side and ruin other patterns!)

Keep these `PROCESS` journals nearby so you will always be able to record your ideas before they escape that beautiful mind of yours! If you have a favorite stitch be sure to check out our other Beading Journals for each particular stitch. Whether you use peyote, brick or loom/square stitch, we've got a `PROCESS` journal for you.

Collect them all!

Have fun beading!
Let that creative genius flow..........

Table of Contents

LOOM/SQUARE STITCH
with round beads

NOTES

NOTES

NOTES

NOTES

NOTES

NOTES

NOTES

NOTES

NOTES

PROJECT_____   DATE _____

NOTES

NOTES

NOTES

NOTES

NOTES

NOTES

NOTES

NOTES

NOTES

NOTES

NOTES

NOTES

NOTES

NOTES

NOTES

NOTES

NOTES

NOTES

NOTES

NOTES

NOTES

NOTES

NOTES

NOTES

NOTES

NOTES

NOTES

NOTES

NOTES

PROJECT_____   DATE _____

NOTES

NOTES

NOTES